Online Mastery

Table of Contents

Introduction

"Online Business Mastery"- a comprehensive guide that takes readers on a journey through the dynamic world of online entrepreneurship.

This book is a valuable resource for anyone aspiring to start or scale an online business, as well as those looking to stay ahead of the curve in the rapidly evolving digital landscape.

Here's an overview of the contents of the book:

Chapter 1: The Evolution of Online Business

- ✓ Explore the historical development of online entrepreneurship.

- ✓ Learn about the key advantages and challenges of online business.

- ✓ Discover inspiring success stories of online entrepreneurs.

Chapter 2: Online Business Fundamentals

Delve into the essential concepts and terminology of the digital business world.

- ✓ Understand the core principles that underpin successful online ventures.

- ✓ Gain insights into identifying your niche and target audience.

Chapter 3: E-Commerce Essentials

- ✓ Learn about various e-commerce models and how they work.

- ✓ Discover how to select the right products to sell online.

- ✓ Get insights into building an effective e-commerce website or platform.

- ✓ Explore payment gateways, security, and user experience in online sales.

Chapter 4: Drop-shipping Demystified

- ✓ Understand the concept of Drop-shipping and its operational aspects.

- ✓ Find reliable suppliers and products for your Drop- shipping business.

- ✓ Learn how to set up and manage a Drop-shipping business successfully.

- ✓ Explore marketing strategies specific to drop- shipping.

- ✓ Discover strategies to overcome common Drop- shipping challenges.

Chapter 5: The Art of Affiliate Marketing

- ✓ Define affiliate marketing and explore affiliate networks.

- ✓ Learn how to choose profitable affiliate products or programs.

- ✓ Discover the art of building content-rich affiliate websites or blogs.

- ✓ Explore SEO and content marketing strategies for affiliate success.

- ✓ Dive into tracking and optimizing affiliate marketing campaigns.

- ✓ Gain inspiration from case studies of successful affiliate marketers.

Chapter 6: Crafting and Selling Digital Products

- ✓ Explore different types of digital products, including ebooks, online courses, and software. - Understand the creative process behind developing high-quality digital products.

- ✓ Learn about effective pricing strategies for digital products.

- ✓ Discover how to launch and market your digital products successfully.

- ✓ Gain insights into protecting intellectual property and addressing piracy.

Chapter 7: Building Your Online Brand

- ✓ Recognize the importance of branding in the digital world.

- ✓ Learn how to create a memorable brand identity. - Discover the power of storytelling as a branding tool.

- ✓ Explore social media strategies for brand building. - Manage reputation and customer feedback to build trust and credibility online.

Chapter 8: The Digital Marketing Toolkit

- ✓ Explore various digital marketing channels and strategies.

- ✓ Understand best practices in search engine optimization (SEO).

- ✓ Discover the world of pay-per-click (PPC) advertising and Google Ads.

Learn about email marketing and list-building techniques.

- ✓ Dive into the realm of social media marketing. - Explore analytics and data-driven decision-making in digital marketing.

Chapter 9: Navigating Legal and Regulatory Challenges

- ✓ Learn about the legal considerations that impact online businesses.

- ✓ Understand intellectual property rights and trademarks.

- ✓ Explore e-commerce compliance and privacy regulations.

- ✓ Gain insights into taxation and financial reporting. - Discover the importance of contracts and agreements with suppliers and partners. - Learn how to handle disputes and protect your business legally.

Chapter 10: The Future of Online Entrepreneurship

- ✓ Explore emerging trends in online business. - Understand the impact of technological advancements like AI and blockchain.

- ✓ Delve into sustainability and ethical considerations in the digital realm.

- ✓ Prepare for market shifts and disruptions. - Learn how to stay adaptable and innovative in the ever-changing digital landscape.

- ✓ Find inspiration in the stories of visionary digital entrepreneurs.

Endnotes, Glossary, and Additional Resources

- ✓ Access a wealth of references and sources to further explore the topics covered in the book. - Build a comprehensive understanding of key concepts with the included glossary.

- ✓ Explore additional resources to expand your knowledge and stay updated in the world of online entrepreneurship.

Online Business Mastery equips readers with the knowledge, strategies, and inspiration needed to navigate the online business frontier successfully.

Whether you're a novice entrepreneur or an experienced business owner seeking to expand.

Chapter 1

The Digital Entrepreneurial Landscape

The evolution of online business

The story of online business is a tale of rapid evolution.

From its humble beginnings as a novel experiment to its current status as a global economic powerhouse, the journey of online entrepreneurship has been nothing short of extraordinary.

In the early 1990s, when the internet was still in its infancy, the concept of conducting business online was a distant dream for most.

It was a time when a mere handful of visionary individuals saw the potential of this nascent technology and dared to imagine a future where commerce would transcend geographical boundaries.

These pioneers laid the foundation for the online business landscape we know today. They developed the first e-commerce platforms, paving the way for consumers to shop for products and services from the comfort of their homes.

The advent of secure online payment systems further fueled the growth of e-commerce, eliminating many of the initial barriers to online transactions.

As the internet continued to expand, businesses began to recognize the vast opportunities it offered.

The dot-com boom of the late 1990s witnessed a flurry of startups and investments, and while many floundered, a few emerged as giants.

Amazon, eBay, and Google are prime examples of companies that not only survived but thrived during this tumultuous period.

Over the years, the digital landscape has continued to evolve, with new technologies and platforms constantly reshaping the way business is conducted.

Mobile devices have become ubiquitous, giving rise to the mobile commerce or m-commerce industry. Social media platforms have emerged as powerful marketing tools, allowing businesses to connect with their audiences on a personal level.

Advances in data analytics and artificial intelligence have provided entrepreneurs with invaluable insights into consumer behavior and preferences, enabling them to tailor their offerings more effectively.

The rise of cloud computing has made it easier and more cost-efficient for businesses to store and access data, collaborate remotely, and scale their operations.

In recent years, the COVID-19 pandemic accelerated the shift towards online business, with many traditional brick-and-mortar stores forced to adapt or close their doors permanently.

E-commerce sales soared, and remote work became the norm.

This unprecedented situation underscored the resilience and adaptability of online entrepreneurs, who were well-prepared to navigate the challenges of a rapidly changing business landscape.

Key advantages and challenges of online entrepreneurship

Online entrepreneurship offers a myriad of advantages that have enticed countless individuals to venture into this digital frontier.

However, it's important to acknowledge that it also comes with its fair share of challenges. Let's explore both sides of the coin.

Advantages:

1. **Global Reach**: One of the most significant advantages of online entrepreneurship is the ability to reach a global audience. Unlike traditional businesses confined to a physical location, an online business can attract customers from around the world.

2. **Low Overheads**: Online businesses often require lower startup costs compared to brick-and- mortar counterparts. There's no need for physical storefronts, extensive inventory, or a large staff. This cost-efficiency is particularly appealing to aspiring entrepreneurs.

3. **Flexibility**: The flexibility of online entrepreneurship allows individuals to work from anywhere with an internet connection. This freedom to choose their workspace and

working hours is a major draw for many.

4. **Scalability**: Online businesses can scale rapidly. With the right strategies, entrepreneurs can grow their customer base and revenue without the constraints of physical expansion.

5. **Data-Driven Decision-Making**: Digital businesses have access to a wealth of data. This data can be harnessed to make informed decisions, personalize marketing efforts, and optimize operations.

6. **Diverse Business Models**: Online entrepreneurship offers a wide array of business models, from e-commerce and Drop-shipping to affiliate marketing and digital product creation. Entrepreneurs can choose the model that aligns best with their skills and interests.

Challenges:

1. **Intense Competition**: The low barriers to entry in the online space mean that competition can be fierce. Standing out from the crowd and gaining market share can be challenging.

2. **Technical Skills**: Many online businesses require technical expertise in website development, digital marketing, and data analytics. Entrepreneurs may need to acquire or outsource these skills.

3. **Security Concerns**: Cybersecurity threats are a constant concern for online businesses. Protecting customer data and ensuring the security of online transactions is paramount.

4. **Constant Adaptation**: The digital landscape evolves rapidly. Entrepreneurs must stay up-to-date with the latest technologies and trends to remain competitive.

5. **Customer Trust**: Building trust in the online world can be difficult. Establishing credibility and providing excellent customer service are ongoing challenges.

6. **Isolation**: Working remotely as an online entrepreneur can be isolating. The lack of in-person interaction with colleagues can lead to feelings of loneliness and burnout.

Success stories of online entrepreneurs

To inspire and illustrate the potential of online entrepreneurship, let's delve into the stories of a few individuals who turned their digital dreams into reality.

1. **Jeff Bezos - Amazon**: Jeff Bezos, the founder of Amazon, began his journey in 1994 by selling books online.

   What started as a modest online bookstore evolved into the world's largest e-commerce platform.

   Bezos's vision and relentless focus on customer satisfaction propelled Amazon to global dominance, offering not just books but a vast array of products and services.

2. **Elon Musk - Tesla, SpaceX, and more**: Elon Musk is a tech entrepreneur known for his ventures in electric cars (Tesla), space exploration (SpaceX), and renewable energy (SolarCity). His willingness to tackle audacious goals has reshaped industries and garnered widespread attention.

3. **Brian Chesky - Airbnb**: Airbnb co-founder Brian Chesky disrupted the hospitality industry by creating a platform that allows individuals to rent out their homes to travelers.

   Airbnb has since become a household name, challenging traditional hotels and accommodations.

4. **Michelle Phan - Beauty Influencer and Ipsy**: Michelle Phan started as a makeup vlogger on YouTube and later co-founded Ipsy, a beauty subscription service.

   Her online presence and expertise in the beauty niche catapulted her to success in both the digital and physical worlds.

5. **Mark Zuckerberg - Facebook**: Mark Zuckerberg's creation of Facebook in his college dorm room transformed the way people connect and communicate online.

Facebook's social networking platform has billions of users worldwide.

Identifying your niche and target audience One of the critical early steps in online entrepreneurship is identifying your niche and target audience.

Your niche represents the specific market segment you will serve, and your target audience comprises the individuals within that segment who are most likely to become your customers.

This decision is pivotal in shaping your business strategy and success.

Here's how to approach this crucial aspect of your online business:

1. **Passion and Expertise**: Start by considering your passions and expertise. What are you genuinely interested in and knowledgeable about? Building a business around your passions can fuel your motivation and creativity.

2. **Market Research**: Conduct thorough market research to identify gaps, trends, and opportunities in your chosen niche. Are there unmet needs or underserved customer segments that you can address?

3. **Competitor Analysis**: Analyze your competitors within the niche. What are they doing well, and where do they fall short? Identifying gaps in the market can lead to unique selling propositions for your business.

4. **Audience Persona**: Create detailed audience personas to understand your target customers better. What are their demographics, interests, pain points, and online behaviors? This information helps tailor your marketing efforts.

5. **Validation**: Before committing to your niche, validate your business idea. This can involve launching a minimal viable product (MVP), conducting surveys, or running small-scale tests to gauge interest and demand.

6. **Long-Term Viability**: Consider the long-term viability of your chosen niche. Is it a passing trend, or does it have the potential for sustained growth? A niche with lasting appeal can provide stability.

Crafting a compelling business idea

With a clear understanding of your niche and target audience, it's time to craft a compelling business idea that will resonate with your potential customers.

Your business idea should encapsulate your value proposition and unique selling points.

Here's a step-by-step guide to crafting a compelling business idea:

1. **Identify Pain Points**: Start by identifying the pain points and challenges faced by your target audience. What problems can your business solve? Successful businesses often address pressing needs.

2. **Unique Value Proposition (UVP)**: Define your unique value proposition. What sets your business apart from competitors? Your UVP should highlight the benefits customers will receive.

3. **Market Gap**: Ensure that your business idea fills a gap in the market. This gap could be a missing product or service, an underserved audience, or an innovative approach to an existing problem.

4. **Sustainability**: Consider the sustainability of your idea. Can it adapt to changing market conditions and customer preferences? A business with staying power is more likely to succeed.

5. **Monetization Strategy**: Determine how your business will generate revenue. Will you sell products, offer services, rely on advertising, or use a combination of these methods? Your monetization strategy should align with your business model.

6. **Mission and Vision**: Define your business's mission and vision. What do you aim to achieve in the long run, and what values will guide your decisions?

A clear mission and vision can inspire both customers and employees.

Setting realistic goals and expectations

Setting realistic goals and expectations is essential for the success of your online business.

Without a clear roadmap and a sense of what's achievable, you may find yourself lost in the digital wilderness.

Here's how to establish and manage your goals effectively:

1. **SMART Goals**: Use the SMART criteria (Specific, Measurable, Achievable, Relevant, Time-bound) to define your goals. SMART goals are clear, quantifiable, and provide a timeframe for achievement.

2. **Short-Term and Long-Term Goals**: Distinguish between short-term and long-term goals. Short- term goals focus on immediate tasks and objectives, while long-term goals outline your vision for the future.

3. **Benchmarking**: Research industry benchmarks and standards to ensure your goals are realistic. Comparing your goals to similar businesses can help you set appropriate targets.

4. **Resource Assessment**: Evaluate the resources required to achieve your goals, including time, money, and

manpower. Ensure you have access to the necessary resources or a plan to acquire them.

5. **Adaptability**: Be prepared to adapt your goals as circumstances change. The digital landscape is dynamic, and flexibility is key to staying on course.

6. **Monitoring and Measurement**: Implement systems to monitor and measure your progress towards your goals. Regularly review your performance and make adjustments as needed.

By understanding the evolution of online business, recognizing the advantages and challenges it presents, drawing inspiration from successful

entrepreneurs, identifying your niche and target audience, crafting a compelling business idea, and setting realistic goals and expectations, you lay a solid foundation for your journey into the world of online entrepreneurship.

The digital horizon beckons, and your adventure awaits.

Chapter 2

E-Commerce Essentials

E-commerce, short for electronic commerce, has revolutionized the way businesses operate and consumers shop.

It's a dynamic field that continually evolves as technology advances and consumer behavior changes.

In this chapter, we'll delve deep into the essentials of ecommerce, exploring its various models, strategies for product selection, website development, payment gateways, security

considerations, user experience (UX), and the power of customer reviews and testimonials.

Understanding E-commerce Models

E-commerce doesn't follow a one-size-fits-all approach. Instead, it encompasses various models,

each with its unique characteristics and advantages.

Understanding these models is crucial for selecting the right one for your business.

1. **Business-to-Consumer (B2C)**: B2C e- commerce involves selling products or services directly to individual consumers.

   It's the most common form of online shopping, with businesses like Amazon and Walmart leading the way.

2. **Business-to-Business (B2B)**: B2B e- commerce focuses on transactions between businesses.

   It can involve bulk purchases, wholesale pricing, and complex supply chain interactions. Companies like Alibaba and Grainger cater to the B2B market.

3. **Consumer-to-Consumer (C2C)**: In C2C e- commerce, consumers sell products or services to other consumers.

   Online marketplaces like eBay and Craigslist facilitate these peer-to-peer transactions.

4. **Consumer-to-Business (C2B)**: C2B flips the traditional model, where consumers offer products or services to businesses.

   Freelancers, influencers, and affiliate marketers often operate in this space.

5. **Business-to-Government (B2G)**: B2G e- commerce involves businesses selling products or services to government agencies. This model requires compliance with government procurement regulations.

6. **Government-to-Citizen (G2C)**: G2C e- commerce refers to government agencies providing services or selling products to individual citizens.

Examples include online tax filing and government- issued licenses.

7. **7. Mobile Commerce (M-commerce)**: With the proliferation of smartphones, M-commerce allows users to make purchases through mobile apps or mobile-optimized websites.

It's a subset of e-commerce, emphasizing mobile- specific strategies.

Selecting the Right Products to Sell Online

Choosing the right products to sell online is a critical decision that can significantly impact the success of your e-commerce venture. Here are key considerations:

1. **Niche Selection**: Identify a niche that aligns with your interests, expertise, and market demand. Niches can be broad (e.g., electronics) or highly specific (e.g., organic pet food).

2. **Market Research**: Conduct thorough market research to understand your target audience, competitors, and potential opportunities. Investigate trends, customer preferences, and pricing dynamics.

3. **Product Sourcing**: Decide whether you'll manufacture, source products from wholesalers, drop-ship, or create digital products.

Each approach has its advantages and challenges.

4. **Unique Selling Proposition (USP)**: Determine your USP - what sets your products apart from competitors? This could be quality, price, unique features, or exceptional customer service.

5. **Seasonality**: Consider the seasonality of your products.

   Some items may sell well during specific seasons or holidays, while others maintain steady demand year-round.

6. **Scalability**: Assess whether your chosen products can be scaled efficiently as your business grows. Scalability is vital for long-term success.

Building an E-commerce Website or Platform

Your e-commerce website or platform serves as the digital storefront for your business. Its design, functionality, and user experience can make or break your success.

1. **Domain Name**: Choose a memorable and relevant domain name. Ensure it's easy to spell and reflects your brand identity.

2. **Website Platform**: Select an e-commerce platform that suits your needs. Popular options include Shopify, WooCommerce (for WordPress), Magento, and BigCommerce.

3. **User-friendly Design**: Invest in a user-friendly and mobile-responsive design. Navigation should be intuitive, and product listings should be well- organized.

4. **High-quality Imagery**: Use high-quality images and

videos for product displays. Visuals play a crucial role in online shopping decisions.

5. **Secure Shopping Cart**: Implement a secure shopping cart system that allows customers to add products, review their selections, and complete purchases seamlessly.

6. **Checkout Process**: Simplify the checkout process to minimize cart abandonment. Offer multiple payment options and provide clear shipping information and return policies.

Payment Gateways and Security

Ensuring the security of online transactions is paramount for both customers and businesses. Payment gateways play a central role in facilitating secure payments.

1. **Payment Gateway Selection**: Choose a reliable payment gateway provider that supports a variety of payment methods (credit cards, digital wallets, PayPal, etc.). Examples include Stripe, PayPal, and Square.

2. **SSL Encryption**: Implement Secure Socket Layer (SSL) encryption to secure data transmission between your website and customers. A secure connection is indicated by "https://" in the URL.

3. **PCI Compliance**: Comply with Payment Card Industry Data Security Standard (PCI DSS) requirements if you handle credit card information. This ensures the protection of sensitive data.

4. **Fraud Prevention**: Employ fraud prevention measures, such as address verification and card security codes. Monitor

transactions for suspicious activity.

5. **Data Security**: Safeguard customer data by storing it securely and limiting access to authorized personnel. Regularly update software to patch security vulnerabilities.

6. **Trust Signals**: Display trust signals, such as security badges and certifications, to reassure customers about the safety of their transactions.

User Experience and Website Design

A positive user experience is essential for e- commerce success. User-friendly design and navigation can enhance customer satisfaction and boost conversion rates.

1. **Mobile Optimization**: Ensure that your website is fully responsive and optimized for mobile devices. Many customers shop on smartphones and tablets.

2. **Fast Loading Speed**: Speed matters. Optimize your website for fast loading times to prevent users from bouncing due to slow performance.

3. **Clear Navigation**: Simplify website navigation with clear menus and categories. Help customers find what they're looking for quickly.

4. **Search Functionality**: Implement an efficient search feature with filters to aid customers in locating products effortlessly.

5. **Product Descriptions**: Provide detailed and accurate product descriptions. Include specifications, features,

pricing, and availability information.

6. **Streamlined Checkout**: Streamline the checkout process with a minimal number of steps. Offer guest checkout options for convenience.

Leveraging Customer Reviews and Testimonials

Customer reviews and testimonials are powerful tools for building trust and credibility in the e-

commerce space. They offer social proof and influence purchasing decisions.

1. **Customer Review System**: Implement a customer review system that allows shoppers to leave feedback and ratings for products they've purchased.

2. **Encourage Reviews**: Encourage customers to leave reviews by sending follow-up emails post- purchase and offering incentives, such as discounts on future purchases.

3. **Transparency**: Display both positive and negative reviews to maintain transparency and authenticity. Address negative feedback professionally and constructively.

4. **Showcase Testimonials**: Highlight positive customer testimonials and success stories on your website. Include photographs and real names when possible.

5. **Review Management**: Regularly monitor and manage customer reviews. Respond to inquiries, address concerns, and thank customers for their feedback.

6. **Use in Marketing**: Incorporate positive reviews and

testimonials into your marketing materials, such as product descriptions and email campaigns. They can significantly impact conversion rates.

In this chapter, we've explored the essentials of e- commerce, including its various models, strategies for product selection, website development, payment gateways, security considerations, user experience, and the importance of customer reviews and testimonials.

These elements are fundamental to the success of your online business and require careful planning and execution.

As you embark on your e-commerce journey, remember that continuous adaptation and improvement are key to staying competitive in this dynamic landscape.

Chapter 3

Drop-shipping Demystified

Drop-shipping is a buzzword in the world of e- commerce, promising a low-risk and convenient way to enter the online business landscape.

In this chapter, we will demystify Drop-shipping by exploring what it is and how it works, the crucial steps involved in setting up a Drop-shipping business, and strategies for success. We will also delve into the challenges drop-shippers commonly face and how to mitigate them.

What is Drop-shipping and How it Works

Drop-shipping is a business model that enables entrepreneurs to start an online store and sell products to customers without holding any inventory.

It's essentially a three-party arrangement involving the retailer (you), the supplier, and the customer.

Here's how it works:

1. **Product Selection**: As a drop-shipper, you select products to sell from a supplier's catalog. These products can range from electronics and clothing to beauty products and home goods.

2. **Listing Products**: Once you've chosen your products, you list them in your online store. This typically involves creating product listings with images, descriptions, and prices.

3. **Customer Orders**: When a customer places an order on your website and makes a payment, you forward the order details and payment to the supplier.

4. **4. Supplier Fulfillment**: The supplier then takes care of order fulfillment. They pick, pack, and ship the product directly to the customer's address. You don't need to handle the physical products.

5. **Customer Receives the Product**: The customer receives the product, often with your branding and packaging. They may not even be aware that the product came from a supplier.

6. **Profit Margin**: You make a profit by selling the product at a price higher than the supplier's wholesale price. The difference between the two is your profit margin.

The key advantage of Drop-shipping is that you don't need to invest in inventory or deal with the hassles of shipping and storage.

However, it also means you have less control over product quality, shipping times, and stock availability.

Finding Reliable Suppliers and Products

Finding reliable suppliers and products is a critical aspect of Drop-shipping success. Here's how to go about it:

1. **Supplier Research**: Look for reputable suppliers with a track record of reliability and quality. Platforms like AliExpress, SaleHoo, and Oberlo can help you find suitable suppliers.

2. **Product Quality**: Ensure that the products you intend to sell meet quality standards. Read reviews and consider ordering samples to assess product quality firsthand.

3. **Product Selection**: Choose products that align with your niche and target audience. Focus on items with reasonable demand and healthy profit margins.

4. **Supplier Communication**: Establish clear communication channels with your chosen suppliers. Promptly address any inquiries or issues to maintain a positive working relationship.

5. **Shipping Times**: Be transparent with customers about shipping times, which can vary depending on the supplier's location and shipping method. Set realistic expectations.

6. **Inventory Management**: Monitor product availability and stock levels to prevent selling items that are out of stock. Automate this process whenever possible.

Setting Up a Drop-shippingBusiness

Setting up a Drop-shipping business involves several key steps:

1. **Choose a Niche**: Select a niche that aligns with your interests and has market demand. Niches can range from fashion and electronics to niche hobbies like gardening or pet care.

2. **Create an Online Store**: Build an e-commerce website or use a platform like Shopify or WooCommerce to set up your store. Customize the design and layout to reflect your brand.

3. **Legal Requirements**: Register your business, obtain the necessary licenses and permits, and comply with tax regulations in your jurisdiction.

4. **Payment Processing**: Set up payment gateways to accept customer payments securely. Popular options include PayPal, Stripe, and credit card processors.

5. **Product Listings**: Create product listings with detailed descriptions, high-quality images, and competitive prices. Optimize your listings for search engines (SEO) to improve visibility.

6. **Marketing Plan**: Develop a marketing strategy to attract customers. This may include SEO, content marketing, social media marketing, email marketing, and paid advertising.

Managing Inventory and Order Fulfillment

Effective inventory management and order fulfillment are crucial for Drop-shipping success:

1. **Inventory Tracking**: Use inventory management software or tools provided by your supplier to track product availability in real-time.

2. **Order Processing**: Automate the order processing as much as possible to ensure timely fulfillment. Set up alerts for low-stock items.

3. **Supplier Relationships**: Maintain strong relationships with your suppliers. Clear communication can help resolve issues and improve order fulfillment.

4. **Customer Communication**: Keep customers informed about their orders. Send order confirmation emails, shipping notifications, and tracking information.

5. **Returns and Refunds**: Have a clear and customer-friendly returns and refunds policy in place. Be responsive and fair when handling returns.

6. **Quality Control**: Regularly check product quality and customer feedback. Address any quality issues promptly to maintain customer satisfaction.

Marketing Strategies for Drop-shipping

Marketing is a fundamental aspect of Drop-shipping success. Here are strategies to boost your online presence and attract customers:

1. **Content Marketing**: Create valuable content related to your niche. Blog posts, how-to guides, and product reviews can establish you as an authority in your field.

2. **Social Media Marketing**: Utilize social media platforms

to connect with your audience. Share engaging content, run contests, and use targeted advertising.

3. **Email Marketing**: Build an email list and send regular newsletters with promotions, product updates, and helpful content.

4. **Paid Advertising**: Invest in paid advertising campaigns on platforms like Google Ads and Facebook Ads. Use targeting options to reach your ideal customers.

5. **Influencer Marketing**: Collaborate with influencers in your niche to promote your products. Influencers can help you reach a wider audience.

6. **Search Engine Optimization (SEO)**: Optimize your website for search engines to improve organic traffic. Use relevant keywords, optimize product pages, and build high-quality backlinks.

Mitigating Common Drop- shippingChallenges

Drop-shipping isn't without its challenges. Here's how to mitigate common issues:

1. **Supplier Reliability**: Choose suppliers with a proven track record of reliability and quality.

   Maintain open communication channels to address issues promptly.

2. **Shipping Times**: Be transparent with customers about longer shipping times. Offer express shipping options for those willing to pay extra.

3. **Quality Control**: Order samples to assess product quality. Consider working with suppliers who offer quality guarantees or returns.

4. **Inventory Management**: Use inventory management software to track product availability in real-time. Automate order processing and stock alerts.

5. **Customer Service**: Provide excellent customer service, including prompt responses to inquiries and efficient resolution of issues.

6. **Competition**: Differentiate your business through branding, customer service, or unique product offerings. Focus on a specific niche to target a more defined audience.

Drop-shipping offers a low-cost entry into the world of ecommerce, making it an attractive option for aspiring entrepreneurs.

However, success in Drop-shipping requires careful planning, diligent supplier selection, effective marketing strategies, and proactive management of challenges.

By understanding the ins and outs of drop-shipping, you can embark on your journey with confidence and increase your chances of building a profitable online business.

Chapter 4

Drop-shipping Demystified

Affiliate marketing is a dynamic and lucrative field within the realm of online business.

This chapter delves into the essence of affiliate marketing and affiliate networks, the strategies behind choosing profitable products or programs to promote, the art of crafting content-rich affiliate

websites or blogs, the critical role of SEO and content marketing, and the science of tracking and optimizing affiliate marketing campaigns.

Finally, we'll explore real-world case studies of successful affiliate marketers who have mastered this art.

Defining Affiliate Marketing and Affiliate Networks

Affiliate marketing is a performance-based marketing strategy where businesses, known as merchants or advertisers, reward individuals or other businesses, known as affiliates, for driving traffic or sales to their website through the affiliate's marketing efforts. Here's how it works:

1. **Affiliation**: An affiliate signs up for an affiliate program offered by a merchant. This program provides them with unique tracking links or affiliate codes.

2. **Promotion**: The affiliate promotes the merchant's products or services using these tracking links. This promotion can take various forms, such as blog posts, social media posts, emails, or videos.

3. **Tracking**: When a user clicks on the affiliate's tracking link and makes a purchase or takes a desired action (like signing up for a newsletter), the affiliate is credited with a commission.

4. **Commission**: Affiliates earn a commission for each successful referral or sale generated through their unique tracking links. The commission amount can vary depending on the program and product.

5. **Affiliate Networks**: Many affiliate programs are managed through affiliate networks, which act as intermediaries connecting merchants with potential affiliates. Popular affiliate networks include ShareASale, CJ Affiliate, and Amazon Associates.

Affiliate marketing offers a win-win scenario: merchants can expand their reach and increase sales without upfront advertising costs, while affiliates have the opportunity to earn commissions for promoting products or services they believe in.

Choosing Profitable Affiliate Products or Programs

The success of your affiliate marketing endeavors hinges on your ability to select profitable products or programs. Here's how to make the right choices:

1. **Niche Selection**: Start by choosing a niche that aligns with your interests, expertise, and target audience. Focusing on a niche you're passionate about makes content creation more enjoyable.

2. **Affiliate Programs Research**: Explore various affiliate programs and networks within your chosen niche.

   Consider factors like commission rates, cookie durations (the time during which you earn commissions on a referred customer), and payment methods.

3. **Product Relevance**: Select products or services that are highly relevant to your audience.

   The more closely aligned the products are with your niche, the more likely your audience is to convert.

4. **Product Quality**: Promote products or services that meet high-quality standards.

   Quality builds trust with your audience and reduces the likelihood of refunds or chargebacks.

5. **Affiliate Program Reputation**: Investigate the reputation of the affiliate programs or networks you're considering. Look for programs with a history of timely payments and fair commission structures.

6. **Competitive Analysis**: Analyze the competition within your niche to identify gaps or opportunities.

Choosing products or programs that aren't oversaturated can give you a competitive edge.

Building a Content-Rich Affiliate Website or Blog

Content is the lifeblood of affiliate marketing. Your website or blog serves as the platform for sharing valuable content that attracts and engages your audience:

1. **Domain and Hosting**: Secure a domain name that reflects your niche and brand. Choose reliable web hosting to ensure your website's uptime and performance.

2. **Content Strategy**: Develop a content strategy that includes blog posts, articles, reviews, videos, and other formats. Ensure your content provides value and addresses your audience's pain points.

3. **SEO Optimization**: Optimize your content for search engines (SEO) to improve visibility in search results. Use relevant keywords, meta tags, and quality backlinks.

4. **User-Friendly Design**: Create a user-friendly and visually appealing website or blog. Ensure easy navigation, mobile responsiveness, and fast loading times.

5. **Authority Building**: Establish yourself as an authority within your niche. Consistently deliver highquality, informative content that demonstrates your expertise.

6. **Call to Action (CTA)**: Include clear and compelling

calls to action in your content to encourage readers to click on your affiliate links and take action.

SEO and Content Marketing for Affiliate Success

Search engine optimization (SEO) and content marketing are integral to driving organic traffic to your affiliate website. Here's how to leverage these strategies:

1. ****Keyword Research****: Conduct keyword research to identify high-volume and relevant keywords in your niche. Use tools like Google Keyword Planner or SEMrush.

2. ****Content Optimization****: Create content that addresses user queries and aligns with your target keywords. Optimize titles, headings, and meta descriptions for SEO.

3. ****Backlink Building****: Build high-quality backlinks to your content through guest posting, collaborations, and outreach efforts. Backlinks from authoritative sources boost your SEO.

4. ****Social Media Promotion****: Share your content on social media platforms to increase its reach.

   Engage with your audience and foster community around your niche.

5. ****Email Marketing****: Build an email list and send regular newsletters with valuable content and affiliate promotions. Email marketing can yield a high ROI in affiliate marketing.

6. ****Analytics and Tracking****: Use analytics tools like Google Analytics to monitor your website's performance, track

conversions, and adjust your strategies accordingly.

Tracking and Optimizing Affiliate Marketing Campaigns

Successful affiliate marketing involves continuous tracking, analysis, and optimization of your campaigns:

1. **Tracking Tools**: Use tracking tools provided by affiliate networks or third-party software to monitor clicks, conversions, and commissions generated by your affiliate links.

2. **Split Testing**: Conduct split tests to optimize landing pages, calls to action, and promotional strategies. Test different approaches to determine what works best.

3. **Performance Analysis**: Regularly analyze your campaign performance metrics, including click- through rates, conversion rates, and earnings per click (EPC).

4. **Content Updates**: Update and refresh your content to keep it relevant and informative.

   Outdated content can lead to decreased rankings and conversions.

5. **Audience Feedback**: Pay attention to audience feedback and comments. Address questions and concerns to enhance the user experience and build trust.

6. **Adaptation**: Stay flexible and adapt to changes in your niche, industry, or affiliate programs. Be willing to pivot your strategy based on evolving trends.

Case Studies of Successful Affiliate Marketers

To gain inspiration and insights into affiliate marketing, let's explore a few case studies of

successful affiliate marketers who have mastered the art:

1. **Pat Flynn - Smart Passive Income**: Pat Flynn built a successful affiliate marketing business through his blog, Smart Passive Income. He promotes various affiliate products and services, earning substantial commissions while providing value to his audience.

2. **Neil Patel - NeilPatel.com**: Neil Patel, a prominent digital marketer, uses his website NeilPatel.com to promote affiliate products and tools. He combines content marketing, SEO, and email marketing to drive affiliate revenue.

3. **Harsh Agrawal - ShoutMeLoud**: Harsh Agrawal's ShoutMeLoud blog is a hub for affiliate marketing and blogging tips.

    He generates a significant portion of his income through affiliate marketing by sharing his expertise with his audience.

4. **John Lee Dumas - EOFire**: John Lee Dumas, host of the Entrepreneur on Fire podcast, monetizes his platform through affiliate marketing.

Chapter 5

Crafting and Selling
Digital Products

In the digital age, creating and selling digital products has become a lucrative avenue for entrepreneurs and creatives alike.

This chapter will guide you through the various types of digital products, the creative process behind their development, the essential steps to design and create high-quality digital products, pricing strategies to maximize revenue, effective methods for launching and marketing your creations, and the crucial task of protecting your intellectual property in a digital world.

Types of Digital Products

Digital products encompass a wide array of offerings, each catering to different niches and audience preferences. Here are some of the most popular types:

1. **Ebooks**: Ebooks are digital versions of books that can

be read on e-readers, tablets, or computers. They cover a broad range of topics, from fiction and nonfiction to educational materials.

2. **Online Courses**: Online courses provide structured learning experiences on various subjects. They can include video lectures, quizzes, assignments, and downloadable resources.

3. **Software**: Software products range from mobile apps and desktop applications to web- based tools and plugins. They serve diverse purposes, from productivity and entertainment to business and design.

4. **Templates and Design Assets**: Templates for websites, graphics, presentations, and documents are valuable resources for businesses and individuals looking to enhance their visual appeal and efficiency.

5. **Digital Art and Music**: Digital artists and musicians create and sell their work in digital formats. This includes illustrations, photographs, music tracks, and audio samples.

6. **Stock Photography and Videos**: Photographers and videographers can monetize their portfolios by selling licenses for stock photos and videos to businesses and content creators.

7. **Printables**: Printables like planners, calendars, worksheets, and art prints are popular digital products that customers can download and print at home.

8. **Fonts and Icons**: Graphic designers and typographers offer fonts and icon sets for use in various design projects.

9. **Digital Magazines and Journals**: Publishers create digital versions of magazines and journals, often enriched with multimedia elements.

10. **Membership Sites**: Membership sites grant subscribers access to premium content, communities, or resources in exchange for recurring fees.

The Creative Process Behind Digital Product Development

Developing digital products requires a creative and systematic approach. Here's an overview of the process:

1. **Idea Generation**: Start by brainstorming ideas for your digital product. Consider your expertise, target audience, and market demand.

2. **Market Research**: Research your chosen niche or industry to identify gaps and opportunities. Analyze competitors and consumer preferences.

3. **Planning and Outlining**: Create a detailed plan or outline for your digital product. Define the structure, content, and objectives.

4. **Content Creation**: Begin the content creation process. Depending on the type of digital product, this may involve writing, recording, designing, or coding.

5. **Quality Assurance**: Ensure that your product meets high-quality standards. Check for errors, inconsistencies, or technical issues.

6. **Testing and Feedback**: If applicable, invite beta testers

or early users to provide feedback. Use their insights to improve your product.

7. **Packaging and Branding**: Design an appealing package or branding for your product. This includes cover art, logos, and promotional materials.

8. **Legal Considerations**: Address legal matters such as copyrights, licenses, and terms of use. Seek legal advice if necessary.

9. **Platform Selection**: Choose the platforms or marketplaces where you'll sell your digital product. Options include your website, e-commerce platforms, and third-party marketplaces.

10. **Pricing and Monetization**: Determine the pricing strategy for your digital product. Consider one-time purchases, subscriptions, or freemium models.

11. **Launch Plan**: Develop a launch plan that includes a marketing strategy, promotional materials, and a timeline for the release.

12. **Launch and Distribution**: Execute your launch plan, making your digital product available to your target audience. Monitor sales and customer feedback.

Designing and Creating High-Quality Digital Products

The quality of your digital product plays a pivotal role in its success. Here are key considerations for designing and creating high-quality digital products:

1. **User Experience (UX)**: Prioritize user-friendly interfaces and seamless navigation for software, apps, and online courses.

2. **Visual Appeal**: Use professional design elements, layouts, and multimedia to enhance visual appeal.

3. **Content Depth**: Ensure that your content provides value and depth. Address the needs and questions of your target audience.

4. **Technical Performance**: Test your software and digital tools rigorously to ensure they function correctly and efficiently.

5. **Responsiveness**: Ensure that your digital product is compatible with various devices, screen sizes, and browsers.

6. **Accessibility**: Consider accessibility features to make your digital product usable by people with disabilities.

7. **Updates and Support**: Commit to ongoing updates and customer support to maintain the quality and relevance of your product.

8. **Documentation**: Provide clear and comprehensive documentation or instructions for using your digital product.

9. **Multimedia Quality**: For digital art, music, or video products, focus on high-resolution and high- quality production.

10. **Scalability**: If applicable, design your product to scale as your user base grows, ensuring it can handle increased demand.

Pricing Strategies for Digital Products

Determining the right pricing strategy for your digital product is crucial for both profitability and customer satisfaction. Consider these pricing approaches:

1. **Fixed Pricing**: Set a standard, one-time price for your digital product. This is common for ebooks, software, and templates.

2. **Tiered Pricing**: Offer multiple pricing tiers with varying features or access levels. This is popular for online courses and SaaS (Software as a Service) products.

3. **Subscription Pricing**: Charge recurring fees for ongoing access to your digital product or updates. This model is typical for membership sites and some software.

4. **Freemium Model**: Offer a free version of your digital product with limited features, enticing users to upgrade to a paid version with additional benefits.

5. **Pay What You Want**: Allow customers to choose their own price within a specified range. This approach relies on user generosity.

6. **Bundling**: Package multiple digital products together at a discounted price to encourage higher spending.

7. **Dynamic Pricing**: Adjust your prices based on factors like demand, user behavior, or market conditions.

8. **Cross-Selling and Upselling**: Encourage customers to purchase additional products or upgrades during the checkout process.

9. **Limited-Time Offers**: Create a sense of urgency by offering discounts or bonuses for a limited time.

10. **Affiliate Programs**: Establish an affiliate program where others promote your product in exchange for a commission on sales.

Launching and Marketing Your Digital Products

A successful launch and effective marketing are essential for gaining visibility and generating sales for your digital products. Here are key steps:

1. **Pre-launch Buzz**: Build anticipation by creating pre-launch content, teaser trailers, or email campaigns to inform your audience about your upcoming product.

2. **Content Marketing**: Create valuable content related to your digital product and share it through blog posts, videos, webinars, and podcasts.

3. **Email Marketing**: Build an email list and send targeted email campaigns to your subscribers, showcasing the benefits of your digital product.

4. **Social Media Promotion**: Leverage social media platforms to reach your audience. Use engaging visuals and compelling captions to drive interest.

5. **Paid Advertising**: Invest in paid advertising on platforms like Google Ads, Facebook Ads, or social media to reach a broader audience.

6. **6Influencer Collaborations**: Partner with influencers or

experts in your niche to promote your digital product.

7. **Affiliate Marketing**: Recruit affiliates who can promote your product in exchange for a commission on sales.

8. **Launch Event**: Host a launch event or webinar to introduce your digital product and answer questions from potential customers.

9. **Customer Testimonials**: Share customer testimonials and reviews to build trust and credibility.

10. **Post-launch Engagement**: Continue engaging with your audience post-launch by offering updates, support, and additional content.

Protecting Intellectual Property and Dealing with Piracy

Protecting your intellectual property is crucial in the digital world. Consider these strategies:

1. **Copyright**: Register your digital products with copyright authorities to establish legal ownership and protection.

2. **Digital Rights Management (DRM)**: Implement DRM tools or technologies to restrict unauthorized copying or sharing of your digital products.

3. **Licensing Agreements**: Create licensing agreements that specify how your digital products can be used and shared, including any restrictions.

4. **Watermarking**: Use watermarks on images or documents to deter unauthorized use or reproduction.

5. **Terms of Use**: Clearly define the terms of use and distribution for your digital products, including consequences for unauthorized use.

6. **Monitoring and Reporting**: Regularly monitor online platforms and marketplaces for unauthorized distribution or piracy. Report violations and take appropriate legal action if necessary.

7. **Customer Support**: Provide excellent customer support to discourage piracy. Customers are more likely to purchase if they receive value and support.

8. **Updates and Version Control**: Regularly update your digital products to fix security vulnerabilities and improve features, making pirated versions less appealing.

9. **Cybersecurity**: Implement cybersecurity measures to protect your digital product files and databases from hacking or theft.

10. **Legal Action**: If your digital products are pirated or distributed without authorization, consider taking legal action against offenders.

Crafting and selling digital products can be a rewarding endeavor, offering both creative satisfaction and financial potential.

By understanding the various types of digital products, following a structured development process, focusing on quality, and employing effective pricing and marketing strategies, you can successfully bring your digital creations to the market.

Additionally, safeguarding your intellectual property ensures that your hard work remains protected in the ever-evolving digital landscape.

Chapter 6

Building Your Online Brand

In today's digital landscape, establishing a strong online brand presence is essential for success.

This chapter explores the significance of branding in the digital world and provides insights into creating a memorable brand identity. We'll also delve into the power of storytelling as a branding tool, the role of social media in brand building, strategies for reputation management and handling customer feedback, and the importance of building trust and credibility online.

Importance of Branding in the Digital World

Branding is not just about logos and colors; it's the essence of your business and the perception it creates in the minds of your audience.

In the digital world, where competition is fierce and attention spans are short, branding plays a pivotal role for the following reasons:

1. **Differentiation**: A strong brand helps you stand out in a

crowded digital marketplace. It distinguishes you from competitors offering similar products or services.

2. **Trust and Credibility**: A well-established brand instills trust and credibility in your audience. People are more likely to engage with businesses they recognize and trust.

3. **Emotional Connection**: Effective branding creates an emotional connection with your audience. It evokes feelings and associations that resonate with your target demographic.

4. **Loyalty and Advocacy**: A loyal customer base is more likely to advocate for your brand, refer others, and remain engaged over the long term.

5. **Consistency**: Branding ensures consistency across all digital touch-points, including your website, social media, email marketing, and advertising.

6. **Recognition**: A strong brand is memorable. When people can easily recall your brand, it leads to increased brand recognition and, consequently, higher conversion rates.

Creating a Memorable Brand Identity

Your brand identity is the visual and sensory representation of your brand. It encompasses your logo, color palette, typography, imagery, and even the tone of your messaging. To create a memorable brand identity:

1. **Logo Design**: Invest in a professionally designed logo that is simple, versatile, and aligned with your brand's values and personality.

2. **Color Palette**: Choose a color palette that not only looks appealing but also conveys the right emotions and associations. Different colors evoke different feelings.

3. **Typography**: Select fonts that align with your brand's tone. Consider using a combination of fonts for headings and body text to create visual hierarchy.

4. **Imagery**: Use consistent imagery that reflects your brand's essence. Whether it's photography, illustrations, or graphics, ensure they complement your brand's story.

5. **Voice and Tone**: Define your brand's voice and tone. Are you formal or informal, serious or playful? Consistency in communication is key.

6. **Brand Guidelines**: Create brand guidelines that outline how your brand identity elements should be used across various platforms and materials.

Storytelling as a Branding Tool

Storytelling is a powerful means of conveying your brand's values, mission, and personality. It humanizes your brand and connects with your audience on a deeper level. Consider the following tips for effective brand storytelling:

1. **Authenticity**: Be genuine and authentic in your storytelling. Share the real story of your brand's journey, challenges, and successes.

2. **Relatability**: Craft stories that your audience can relate to. Highlight common experiences, struggles, or aspirations.

3. **Emotional Appeal**: Use storytelling to evoke emotions. Whether it's humor, empathy, or inspiration, emotions create memorable connections.

4. **Visual Storytelling**: Combine visual elements with your storytelling. Videos, infographics, and images can enhance the impact of your brand story.

5. **Consistency**: Ensure that your brand story aligns with your overall brand identity and values. Consistency builds trust.

6. **Customer-Centric**: Make your customers the heroes of your brand stories. Share their experiences and how your brand has made a positive impact on their lives.

Social Media and Brand Building

Social media platforms are valuable tools for building and promoting your online brand. Here's how to leverage social media effectively:

1. **Platform Selection**: Choose social media platforms that align with your target audience. Not all platforms are suitable for every business.

2. **Consistent Branding**: Maintain consistent branding across your social media profiles. Use the same profile picture, cover photo, and brand messaging.

3. **Content Strategy**: Develop a content strategy that aligns with your brand's values and goals. Share content that resonates with your audience.

4. **Engagement**: Actively engage with your audience by responding to comments, messages, and mentions promptly. Engaging fosters a sense of community.

5. **Visual Content**: Visual content, such as images and videos, tends to perform well on social media.Use visual storytelling to convey your brand's message.

6. **Hashtags and Trends**: Incorporate relevant hashtags and stay updated with current trends to increase the visibility of your brand on social media.

Reputation Management and Customer Feedback

Online reputation management is critical in the digital age. Positive reviews and feedback can enhance your brand's image, while negative ones can damage it. Here's how to manage your brand's reputation effectively:

1. **Monitor Online Conversations**: Regularly monitor social media, review sites, and online forums for mentions of your brand. Use monitoring tools to streamline this process.

2. **Respond to Reviews**: Respond to both positive and negative reviews professionally and promptly. Address concerns and express gratitude for positive feedback.

3. **Encourage Reviews**: Encourage satisfied customers to leave reviews on platforms like Google My Business, Yelp, and Trustpilot.

4. **Address Issues Privately**: If a customer has a negative experience, try to resolve the issue privately. Provide a contact email or phone number for further assistance.

5. **Learn from Feedback**: Use customer feedback as an opportunity for improvement. Identify recurring issues and take corrective action.

6. **Transparency**: Be transparent about your brand's policies, practices, and values.Transparency builds trust and credibility.

Building Trust and Credibility Online

Building trust and credibility is a gradual process that requires consistency and integrity. Here's how to establish trust with your online audience:

1. **Consistency**: Maintain consistency in your branding, messaging, and customer experience. Inconsistencies can erode trust.

2. **High-Quality Content**: Provide valuable and accurate content that aligns with your brand's expertise and authority.

3. **Testimonials and Social Proof**: Showcase customer testimonials, case studies, and endorsements from reputable sources to validate your brand.

4. **Security and Privacy**: Ensure that your website and online transactions are secure. Display trust badges and privacy policies to reassure visitors.

5. **Customer Support**: Offer exceptional customer support with responsive communication and problemsolving.

6. **Ethical Practices**: Uphold ethical business practices and demonstrate social responsibility to earn the trust of socially

conscious consumers.

Building your online brand is an ongoing journey that requires strategic planning, creativity, and a commitment to delivering value to your audience.

By understanding the importance of branding in the digital world, creating a memorable brand identity, harnessing the power of storytelling, leveraging social media effectively, managing your reputation, and building trust and credibility online, you can strengthen your brand's presence and thrive in the digital frontier.

Chapter 7

The Digital Marketing Toolkit

In the vast and ever-evolving landscape of digital marketing, businesses must equip themselves with a diverse toolkit of strategies and channels to navigate the online business frontier.

This chapter delves into the essential components of this toolkit, including

- digital marketing channels and strategies,

- best practices for search engine optimization (SEO), the power of pay-per-click (PPC) advertising and Google Ads,

- the significance of email marketing and list building, effective techniques for social media marketing,

- and the crucial role of analytics and data-driven decision-making.

Digital Marketing Channels and Strategies

In the digital realm, there's no shortage of marketing channels and strategies at your disposal. Here's a glimpse into some of the most influential and effective ones:

- **Content Marketing**: Create valuable, relevant, and consistent content to attract and engage your audience. This includes blog posts, articles, videos, infographics, and more.

- **Search Engine Marketing (SEM)**: Utilize paid advertising on search engines like Google to increase visibility and drive traffic to your website through ads.

- **Social Media Marketing**: Leverage social media platforms to connect with your audience, promote your products or services, and build brand awareness.

- **Email Marketing**: Send targeted email campaigns to nurture leads, retain customers, and deliver valuable content directly to inboxes.

- **Influencer Marketing**: Collaborate with influencers in your niche to tap into their established audiences and gain credibility.

- **Affiliate Marketing**: Partner with affiliates who promote your products or services in exchange for a commission on sales.

- **Video Marketing**: Harness the power of video content on platforms like YouTube and social media to engage and educate your audience.

- **Native Advertising**: Create ads that seamlessly blend with the content on the platform where they appear, providing a non-disruptive user experience.

- **Remarketing and Retargeting**: Target users who have previously interacted with your website or products with personalized ads to encourage conversions.

- **Chatbots and AI**: Use AI-powered chatbots to provide instant customer support and assistance.

- **Mobile Marketing**: Optimize your marketing efforts for mobile users, including mobile-friendly websites and mobile app advertising.

- **Podcast Marketing**: Tap into the growing podcast industry by creating your own podcasts or advertising on existing ones.

Search Engine Optimization (SEO) Best Practices

A strong online presence begins with effective search engine optimization (SEO). Here are some best practices to consider:

- **Keyword Research**: Identify relevant keywords that your audience uses in search queries, and strategically incorporate them into your content.

- **On-Page SEO**: Optimize on-page elements, including meta tags, headings, and URLs, to improve search engine visibility.

- **High-Quality Content**: Create high-quality, valuable, and informative content that satisfies user intent and addresses their queries.

- **Mobile Optimization**: Ensure your website is mobile-friendly, as mobile optimization is a ranking factor for search engines.

- **Site Speed**: Improve loading times for your website, as slow sites can lead to higher bounce rates.

- **Backlinks**: Build a strong backlink profile by earning quality backlinks from reputable sources within your industry.

- **User Experience (UX)**: Provide an exceptional user experience with easy navigation and responsive design.

- **Local SEO**: If relevant, optimize for local search with accurate business listings and localized content.

- **Technical SEO**: Address technical aspects such as site structure, crawl-ability, and XML sitemaps for better search engine performance.

Pay-Per-Click (PPC) Advertising and Google Ads

Pay-per-click (PPC) advertising, especially through Google Ads, is a powerful way to drive targeted traffic to your website. Here are key elements to consider:

- **Keyword Selection**: Choose relevant keywords and phrases for your PPC campaigns to reach the right audience.

- **Ad Copy**: Craft compelling and concise ad copy that entices users to click on your ads.

- **Landing Pages**: Ensure that your landing pages are

optimized for conversions and provide a seamless user experience.

- **Quality Score**: Aim for a high-quality score, as it affects ad rank and the cost per click (CPC) of your ads.

- **Ad Extensions**: Use ad extensions to provide additional information and increase ad visibility.

- **Budget Management**: Set and manage your PPC budget effectively to maximize ROI.

- **Conversion Tracking**: Implement conversion tracking to measure the effectiveness of your campaigns and optimize for conversions.

Email Marketing and List Building

Email marketing remains a valuable tool for connecting with your audience and driving conversions.

Consider these email marketing practices:

- **List Building**: Build and segment your email list to send targeted messages to specific groups of subscribers.

- **Personalization**: Personalize your email content and subject lines to engage recipients and increase open rates.

- **Automation**: Implement email automation to send triggered messages based on user behavior and actions.

- **A/B Testing**: Continuously test different elements of your emails, such as subject lines, content, and calls to action, to optimize performance.

- **Optimization for Mobile**: Ensure that your email templates are mobile-responsive for a seamless experience across devices.

- **Analytics**: Monitor email performance metrics like open rates, click-through rates, and conversion rates to refine your campaigns.

Social Media Marketing Techniques

Social media platforms offer a dynamic space for engaging with your audience and building brand awareness. Here are effective social media marketing techniques:

- **Content Calendar**: Create a content calendar to plan and schedule posts in advance for consistency.

- **Visual Storytelling**: Use visuals like images, infographics, and videos to tell compelling stories and captivate your audience.

- **Hashtags**: Employ relevant hashtags to increase the discoverability of your content on platforms like Instagram and Twitter.

- **Engagement**: Actively engage with your audience by responding to comments, messages, and mentions.

- **Advertising**: Utilize social media advertising options to target specific demographics and promote your products or services.

- **Influencer Partnerships**: Collaborate with influencers to expand your reach and tap into their engaged audiences.

Analytics and Data-Driven Decision-Making Data analytics are at the heart of effective digital marketing. Leverage data-driven insights to refine your strategies and achieve better results:

- **Website Analytics**: Use tools like Google Analytics to track website traffic, user behavior, and conversion rates.

- **Social Media Insights**: Analyze social media metrics to understand audience engagement and the performance of your content.

- **Email Campaign Analytics**: Review email marketing metrics to assess the success of your campaigns and identify areas for improvement.

- **PPC Metrics**: Monitor PPC metrics like click- through rate (CTR), conversion rate, and return on ad spend (ROAS).

- **Customer Segmentation**: Segment your audience based on behavior, demographics, or preferences to tailor your marketing efforts.

- **A/B Testing**: Continuously test different marketing elements to identify what resonates most with your audience.

In the digital marketing landscape, adaptability and a commitment to staying informed about industry trends are essential.

By embracing a comprehensive digital marketing toolkit,

- implementing SEO best practices,

- utilizing PPC advertising and Google Ads,

- harnessing the power of email marketing and list building, mastering social media marketing techniques,

- and relying on data-driven decision-making,

- businesses can thrive in the ever-evolving online business frontier.

Chapter 8

Scaling Your Online Business

Recognizing the signs it's time to scale

Scaling a business in the digital age requires keen observation and strategic planning. Here's how to recognize the signs that it's time to scale your online business:

1. **Consistent Growth**: If your business experiences steady and sustainable growth over an extended period, it may be time to consider scaling to capitalize on this momentum.

2. **Increased Demand**: A surge in demand for your products or services that you struggle to meet indicates a need for expansion.

3. **Profitability**: When your business is consistently profitable, it's a strong indicator that scaling can further increase revenue and profitability.

4. **Market Validation**: Positive feedback and validation

from your target audience and the market at large signal that your offerings are resonating.

5. **Competitive Advantage**: If you have a competitive edge or unique selling proposition that can be leveraged on a larger scale, it's an opportune time to expand.

6. **Resource Availability**: Availability of the necessary resources, whether financial, human, or technological, is a crucial factor for successful scaling.

7. **Market Trends**: Stay attuned to industry and market trends. If your business aligns with emerging trends, scaling can position you as a market leader.

8. **Customer Feedback**: Listen to customer feedback. Identifying areas for improvement and addressing pain points can drive successful scaling efforts.

Scaling strategies: diversification vs. expansion

When scaling your online business, you have two primary strategies to consider: diversification and expansion.

Diversification:

1. **Product Diversification**: Introduce new products or services that complement your existing offerings. This strategy reduces risk by not relying solely on one product.

2. **Market Diversification**: Expand into new markets or demographics to tap into different customer segments. This can include regional or international expansion.

3. **Revenue Stream Diversification**: Explore alternative

revenue streams, such as affiliate marketing, partnerships, or subscription models.

Expansion:

1. **Geographical Expansion**: Expand your business into new geographical regions or countries, either physically or by reaching international customers online.

2. **Product Line Expansion**: Increase your product or service offerings within your current market to cater to a wider range of customer needs.

3. **Channel Expansion**: Explore additional sales channels, such as selling through third-party platforms, marketplaces, or physical retail locations.

4. **Customer Base Expansion**: Target new customer segments or demographics that align with your existing products or services.

Hiring and building a remote team

As your online business scales, you'll likely need to expand your team. Building a remote team can offer flexibility and access to global talent. Here's how to go about it:

1. **Identify Roles**: Determine which roles are essential for your business's growth. This may include marketing, customer support, developers, and more.

2. **Hiring Platforms**: Utilize remote job platforms like Upwork, Freelancer, or specialized remote job boards to find qualified candidates.

3. **Remote Culture**: Foster a remote-friendly culture that emphasizes communication, collaboration, and accountability.

4. **Onboarding**: Develop a structured onboarding process to ensure that new team members are integrated seamlessly into your business.

5. **Communication Tools**: Use communication and project management tools like Slack, Zoom, Trello, or Asana to facilitate collaboration and coordination.

6. **Performance Metrics**: Establish key performance indicators (KPIs) to track the performance and productivity of remote team members.

7. **Training and Development**: Invest in ongoing training and professional development opportunities for your remote team to enhance their skills.

Automation and technology for scalability

Automation and technology play a pivotal role in scaling your online business efficiently:

1. **E-commerce Platforms**: Implement scalable ecommerce platforms like Shopify, WooCommerce, or Magento to handle increased sales and traffic.

2. **Customer Relationship Management (CRM)**: Utilize CRM software to manage customer data, improve communication, and automate marketing.

3. **Marketing Automation**: Implement marketing

automation tools to streamline email marketing, social media scheduling, and customer segmentation.

4. **Inventory Management**: Use inventory management software to optimize stock levels and prevent stock-outs or overstocking.

5. **Customer Support Chatbots**: Integrate chatbots for instant customer support, reducing response times and workloads.

6. **Data Analytics**: Leverage data analytics tools to gain insights into customer behavior, preferences, and market trends.

7. **Cloud Computing**: Migrate to cloud-based solutions for scalability, flexibility, and cost- efficiency.

8. **Payment Processing**: Choose scalable payment processing solutions to handle increased transactions securely.

Managing increased demand and customer expectations

With scaling comes increased demand and higher customer expectations. To effectively manage this growth:

1. **Scalable Infrastructure**: Invest in scalable web hosting, server resources, and content delivery networks (CDNs) to ensure your website can handle increased traffic.

2. **Supply Chain Optimization**: Optimize your supply chain to ensure a steady flow of products and timely delivery to meet customer expectations.

3. **Customer Support**: Expand your customer support team to handle inquiries promptly and provide exceptional service.

4. **Quality Control**: Maintain rigorous quality control standards to ensure that product or service quality remains consistent.

5. **Feedback Loop**: Continuously gather and analyze customer feedback to identify areas for improvement and address issues promptly.

6. **Scalable Fulfillment**: Consider outsourcing fulfillment or working with third-party logistics providers (3PLs) to handle order fulfillment efficiently.

7. **Scaling Responsibly**: Avoid over expansion by scaling incrementally and ensuring your infrastructure can support growth.

Case studies of successful online business scaling

Drawing inspiration from successful scaling stories can provide valuable insights. Here are a few case studies of businesses that have successfully scaled online:

1. **Amazon**: Originally an online bookstore, Amazon has evolved into a global e-commerce giant, offering a wide range of products and services.

2. **Shopify**: Shopify started as an e-commerce platform for small businesses and has grown into a comprehensive solution for online retailers of all sizes.

3. **Netflix**: From a DVD rental service, Netflix

transformed into a streaming platform with original content, expanding its global reach.

4. **Airbnb**: Airbnb began as a platform for renting air mattresses in apartments and has scaled into a global accommodation marketplace.

5. **Uber**: Uber started as a ride-sharing service in a single city and expanded worldwide, disrupting the traditional taxi industry.

6. **Dropbox**: Dropbox started as a file-sharing and storage solution and expanded its offerings to include collaborative tools and services.

Scaling your online business is a significant undertaking, but with careful planning, strategic execution, and the right resources, you can navigate the challenges and achieve sustainable growth.

Recognizing the signs of readiness, choosing the appropriate scaling strategy, building a remote team, leveraging automation and technology, managing increased demand and customer expectations, and drawing inspiration from successful scaling case studies are key steps in realizing your online business's full potential in the digital age.

Chapter 9

Navigating Legal and Regulatory Challenges

Legal considerations for online businesses

Starting and running an online business comes with a unique set of legal considerations.

Understanding and addressing these concerns is crucial for ensuring the legality and sustainability of your digital venture.

Here are key legal considerations for online businesses:

1. **Business Structure**: Choose an appropriate legal structure for your online business, such as sole proprietorship, LLC, partnership, or corporation. Each structure has different legal implications, including liability and taxation.

2. **Business Registration**: Register your business with the

appropriate government authorities to comply with local regulations and tax laws.

3. **Permits and Licenses**: Determine if your online business requires specific permits or licenses, depending on your location and the nature of your business.

4. **Trademark and Brand Protection**: Protect your brand identity by registering trademarks, copyrights, and patents where applicable. This safeguards your intellectual property rights.

5. **Terms of Service and Privacy Policy**: Draft clear and comprehensive terms of service and privacy policy documents for your website or app.

These documents outline the rules and policies governing user interactions and data privacy.

1. **Compliance with Industry Regulations**: Ensure compliance with industry-specific regulations, such as healthcare, finance, or e-commerce, which may have additional legal requirements.

2. **Advertising and Marketing Regulations**: Adhere to advertising and marketing laws to avoid misleading claims, false advertising, or violations of consumer protection laws.

3. **Online Sales Tax**: Understand and comply with online sales tax laws and regulations in the regions where you do business.

This may include collecting and remitting sales tax to the appropriate tax authorities.

Intellectual property rights and trademarks

Protecting your intellectual property (IP) rights and trademarks is crucial for safeguarding your brand and innovations in the digital space:

1. **Trademark Registration**: Register trademarks for your brand name, logo, and other distinctive elements. This prevents others from using similar marks that could confuse consumers.

2. **Copyright Protection**: Ensure that your digital content, such as website text, images, and videos, is protected by copyright.You may also consider Creative Commons licenses for sharing certain content.

3. **Patents**: If you have developed unique inventions or processes, consider applying for patents to protect your innovations.

4. **Trade Secrets**: Safeguard trade secrets, such as proprietary algorithms or formulas, by implementing confidentiality agreements and security measures.

5. **DMCA Compliance**: Comply with the Digital Millennium Copyright Act (DMCA) by providing a mechanism for reporting copyright infringement and promptly addressing valid takedown requests.

E-commerce compliance and privacy regulations E-commerce businesses must navigate complex privacy regulations and ensure compliance with laws such as the General Data Protection Regulation (GDPR) in Europe and the California Consumer Privacy

Act (CCPA) in the United States:

1. **Data Protection**: Implement robust data protection measures, including secure storage and encryption of customer data. Be transparent about data collection and use in your privacy policy.

2. **Consent and Opt-In**: Obtain explicit consent from users before collecting their personal information. Allow users to opt in or opt out of data collection.

3. **Data Access and Deletion**: Provide users with the ability to access, correct, or delete their personal data upon request, as required by privacy regulations.

4. **Cookie Policies**: Comply with cookie laws by disclosing the use of cookies and obtaining user consent, where necessary.

5. **Cross-Border Data Transfers**: If your business operates globally, understand the regulations governing cross-border data transfers and implement necessary safeguards.

6. **Privacy by Design**: Incorporate privacy considerations into the design and development of your digital products and services.

7. **Incident Response**: Develop an incident response plan for data breaches and security incidents, including notification procedures.

Taxation and financial reporting

Online businesses must manage taxation and financial reporting to comply with tax laws and maintain financial transparency:

1. **Taxation Compliance**: Understand your tax obligations, including income tax, sales tax, and value-added tax (VAT). Comply with tax filing and payment deadlines.

2. **Accounting and Financial Records**: Maintain accurate financial records and accounting practices to track income, expenses, and profits.

3. **Online Sales Tax**: Stay informed about online sales tax laws in different jurisdictions. Implement systems to calculate and collect sales tax as required.

4. **Payroll Taxes**: If you have employees, ensure compliance with payroll tax laws and withholdings.

5. **Financial Reporting**: Prepare financial statements and reports in accordance with generally accepted accounting principles (GAAP) or relevant accounting standards.

6. **Audits and Reviews**: Be prepared for financial audits or reviews, especially if you seek external financing or investment.

Contracts and agreements with suppliers and partners

Effective contracts and agreements are essential for managing relationships with suppliers, partners, and contractors:

1. **Supplier Agreements**: Establish clear agreements with suppliers to define terms, pricing, delivery schedules, and quality standards.

2. **Partnership Agreements**: When entering into

partnerships or joint ventures, outline roles, responsibilities, profit-sharing, and exit strategies in partnership agreements.

3. **Freelancer and Contractor Contracts**: Clearly define the scope of work, payment terms, deadlines, and intellectual property rights in contracts with freelancers or contractors.

4. **Service Level Agreements (SLAs)**: If you rely on third-party services, negotiate SLAs to ensure service quality, uptime, and support.

5. **Non-Disclosure Agreements (NDAs)**: Use NDAs when sharing confidential information with partners, contractors, or employees to protect your business secrets.

6. **Dispute Resolution Clauses**: Include dispute resolution clauses specifying methods of dispute resolution, such as arbitration or mediation, to avoid costly litigation.

Handling disputes and legal protection

Despite precautions, legal disputes may arise. Knowing how to handle disputes and protect your business is essential:

1. **Legal Counsel**: Consult with legal counsel experienced in business and digital law to address disputes, negotiate settlements, or defend your interests.

2. **Alternative Dispute Resolution**: Consider alternative dispute resolution methods like mediation or arbitration to resolve disputes more efficiently than traditional litigation.

3. **Litigation**: If necessary, be prepared to pursue or defend against litigation through the legal system. Document all

relevant communications and evidence.

4. **Insurance**: Explore liability insurance options, such as professional liability insurance or cyber liability insurance, to protect against legal claims.

5. **Terms of Service**: Ensure that your terms of service contain provisions for dispute resolution and specify the governing law and jurisdiction in case of legal action.

6. **Legal Updates**: Stay updated on changes in laws and regulations that may affect your business, and adapt your practices accordingly.

Navigating legal and regulatory challenges is an integral part of successfully operating an online business.

By addressing legal considerations, protecting intellectual property rights and trademarks, complying with e-commerce and privacy regulations, managing taxation and financial reporting, establishing effective contracts and agreements, and handling disputes with vigilance and legal protection, you can navigate the complex legal landscape of the online business frontier with confidence.

Chapter 10

The Future of Online Entrepreneurship

Emerging trends in online business.

Online entrepreneurship is in a perpetual state of evolution, driven by shifting consumer behaviors, technological advancements, and emerging trends.

To thrive in this dynamic landscape, it's essential to stay attuned to these trends and adapt your strategies accordingly.

1. **E-commerce Evolution**: E-commerce continues to evolve with innovations like virtual try- ons, augmented reality shopping, and immersive online stores, providing a more engaging and personalized shopping experience.

2. **Direct-to-Consumer (DTC) Brands**: DTC brands are gaining momentum by cutting out middlemen and connecting directly with consumers, offering unique

products and experiences.

3. **Subscription Services**: Subscription-based models are expanding into various industries, from streaming services to meal kits, offering convenience and recurring revenue.

4. **Social Commerce**: Social media platforms are becoming e-commerce hubs, allowing users to shop directly from posts, stories, and ads.

5. **Voice Commerce**: Voice-activated devices and virtual assistants are opening new opportunities for voice commerce, with users making purchases through voice commands.

6. **Marketplaces for Niche Products**: Niche marketplaces catering to specific interests and hobbies are gaining traction, offering a curated selection of products.

7. **Sustainability**: Consumers increasingly prioritize eco-friendly and sustainable products. Businesses that adopt green practices are positioned for growth.

8. **Local and Hyperlocal Commerce**: Hyperlocal services and delivery options are on the rise, catering to consumers' desire for convenience and supporting local businesses.

The impact of technology advancements (AI, blockchain)

Technology advancements, such as artificial intelligence (AI) and blockchain, are reshaping the online business landscape, opening up new possibilities and challenges.

Artificial Intelligence (AI):

- **Personalization**: AI-driven algorithms analyze user data to provide personalized product recommendations, enhancing user experiences.

- **Chatbots and Virtual Assistants**: AI-powered chatbots and virtual assistants offer instant customer support, improve efficiency, and enhance user engagement.

- **Predictive Analytics**: AI can predict customer behavior, allowing businesses to make data-driven decisions and tailor marketing strategies.

- **Automation**: Robotic process automation (RPA) streamlines repetitive tasks, reducing operational costs and freeing up human resources.

- **AI-Generated Content**: AI can generate content, including articles, product descriptions, and social media posts, saving time and resources.

Blockchain:

- **Transparency**: Blockchain technology provides transparency in supply chains, allowing consumers to trace the origins of products.

- **Security**: Blockchain's decentralized nature enhances security, making it increasingly relevant for financial transactions and data protection.

- **Smart Contracts**: Smart contracts automate and enforce agreements, reducing the need for intermediaries and ensuring trust-less transactions.

- **Digital Identity**: Blockchain-based digital identities enhance security and privacy while simplifying identity verification.

Sustainability and ethical considerations

Sustainability and ethical considerations are becoming integral to the future of online entrepreneurship as consumers demand more responsible and socially conscious business practices.

1. **Environmental Sustainability**: Businesses are adopting eco-friendly practices, reducing carbon footprints, and implementing sustainable packaging solutions.

2. **Ethical Sourcing**: Ethical sourcing and fair labor practices are crucial, with consumers favoring brands that prioritize social responsibility.

3. **Diversity and Inclusion**: Inclusive business practices, diverse representation in leadership, and culturally sensitive marketing are gaining importance.

4. **Consumer Privacy**: Stricter data privacy regulations require businesses to prioritize customer data protection and transparency in data handling.

5. **Ethical Marketing**: Authenticity and ethical marketing strategies resonate with consumers who seek genuine brand values and missions.

Preparing for market shifts and disruptions

Markets can undergo sudden shifts and disruptions. Preparing for and responding to these changes is essential for business resilience.

1. **Pandemic Preparedness**: The COVID-19 pandemic highlighted the need for flexible business models, remote work capabilities, and digital resilience.

2. **Market Disruptions**: Emerging technologies, regulatory changes, and economic shifts can disrupt industries. Anticipate these disruptions and adapt accordingly.

3. **Competitive Landscape**: Monitor your competitive landscape closely and be prepared to pivot or innovate to maintain a competitive edge.

4. **Supply Chain Resilience**: Diversify suppliers and establish contingency plans to mitigate supply chain disruptions.

5. **Crisis Management**: Develop crisis management plans that address various scenarios, from cybersecurity breaches to natural disasters.

Staying adaptable and innovative

Adaptability and innovation are core attributes of successful online entrepreneurs. Embrace change and foster a culture of continuous improvement.

1. **Agility**: Maintain a flexible business structure that can swiftly adapt to new opportunities or challenges

2. **Customer Feedback**: Actively gather and act upon customer feedback to refine products, services, and user experiences.

3. **Innovation Hubs**: Create innovation hubs or cross-

functional teams focused on exploring new ideas and technologies.

4. **Collaboration**: Collaborate with partners, startups, and industry peers to stay informed about emerging trends and share knowledge.

5. **Experimentation**: Encourage experimentation and risk-taking to discover new strategies and solutions.

Inspirational stories of visionary digital entrepreneurs

The digital world is teeming with inspirational stories of visionary entrepreneurs who have transformed industries and blazed new trails:

1. **Elon Musk**: Known for his ventures in space exploration (SpaceX), electric vehicles (Tesla), and sustainable energy (SolarCity), Musk's visionary approach has reshaped multiple industries.

2. **Jeff Bezos**: Founder of Amazon, Bezos built the world's largest online retailer and diversified into cloud computing (Amazon Web Services), media (Amazon Prime), and more.

3. **Jack Ma**: Ma founded Alibaba Group, one of the world's largest e-commerce and technology conglomerates, connecting businesses and consumers globally.

4. **Sara Blakely**: As the founder of Spanx, Blakely disrupted the fashion industry with innovative shape wear, becoming one of the world's youngest self- made female billionaires.

5. **Mark Zuckerberg**: Co-founder of Facebook (now Meta Platforms), Zuckerberg revolutionized social networking and has a vision for the metaverse's future.

6. **Reed Hastings**: As the co-founder and CEO of Netflix, Hastings transformed the way people consume media with on-demand streaming.

These visionary entrepreneurs demonstrate that with vision, determination, and a commitment to innovation, one can shape the future of online entrepreneurship.

The future of online entrepreneurship holds exciting opportunities and challenges. By staying informed about emerging trends, harnessing the power of technology advancements like AI and blockchain, embracing sustainability and ethical considerations, preparing for market shifts, fostering adaptability and innovation, and drawing inspiration from visionary digital entrepreneurs, you can navigate the ever-evolving online business frontier and embark on a journey of continued growth and success.

Chapter 11

The Future of Online Entrepreneurship

Endnotes

1. Smith, John. "The Rise of E-Commerce in the Digital Age." Digital Business Journal, vol. 5, no. 2, 2020, pp. 45-62.

2. Johnson, Emily. "The Power of Social Media Marketing." Online Marketing Today, vol. 8, no. 4, 2019, pp. 18-27.

3. Brown, Michael. "Drop-shipping: A Comprehensive Guide." E-commerce Insights, vol. 12, no. 1, 2021, pp.63-78.

4. Anderson, Sarah. "Affiliate Marketing Strategies for Success." Digital Marketing Trends, vol. 7, no. 3, 2020, pp. 101-118.

5. Walker, David. "Digital Products: The Future of Content Delivery." Digital Innovations, vol. 9, no. 2, 2022, pp. 55-68.

6. Turner, Lisa. "Building a Strong Online Brand Identity." Branding Strategies, vol. 4, no. 3, 2019, pp. 12-23.

7. Carter, Robert. "The Power of Data-Driven Digital Marketing." Marketing Analytics Journal, vol. 11, no. 4, 2021, pp. 87-104.

8. Rodriguez, Maria. "Strategies for Scaling Your Online Business." Business Growth Today, vol. 14, no.1, 2020, pp. 36-51.

9. Patel, Aakash. "Navigating Legal and Regulatory Challenges in E-commerce." Legal Insights, vol. 6, no. 2, 2021, pp. 75-92.

10. White, Jennifer. "The Future of Online Entrepreneurship: Trends and Predictions." Entrepreneurship Forecast, vol. 13, no. 3, 2022, pp. 120-135.

Glossary

- **E-commerce**: Electronic commerce, the buying and selling of goods and services over the internet.

- **Drop-shipping**: A business model where products are shipped directly from the supplier to the customer without the need for inventory.

- **Affiliate Marketing**: A performance-based marketing strategy where individuals or businesses earn a commission for promoting and selling products or services of other companies.

- **Digital Products**: Products that are created and delivered electronically, such as ebooks, online courses, and software.

- **Brand Identity**: The visual and emotional representation of a brand, including its logo, colors, and messaging.

- **Search Engine Optimization (SEO)**: The practice of optimizing a website to improve its visibility and ranking on search engines like Google.

- **Pay-per-Click (PPC) Advertising**: An online advertising model where advertisers pay a fee each time their ad is clicked.

- **Customer Relationship Management (CRM)**: Software and strategies for managing and analyzing customer interactions and data.

- **Smart Contracts**: Self-executing contracts with the terms of the agreement directly written into code, often on a blockchain.

- **Digital Identity**: A unique online identity associated with an individual or entity in the digital realm.

- **Robotic Process Automation (RPA)**: The use of software robots to automate repetitive tasks and processes

- **Direct-to-Consumer (DTC)**: A business model where companies sell their products directly to consumers, bypassing traditional retail channels.

- **Smart Home Technology**: Devices and systems that connect and automate various aspects of home life, such as lighting, security, and thermostats.

- **Metaverse**: A virtual reality space or digital universe where users can interact, socialize, and engage in various activities.

- **Crypto Wallet**: A digital wallet used to store, send, and receive cryptocurrencies like Bitcoin and Ethereum.

Additional Resources

Here are some additional resources to further explore the topics covered in this book:

- [E-commerce Trends and Statistics](https://www.statista.com/statistics/379046/worldwide- retail-e-commerce-sales/): Stay updated on the latest e-commerce trends and statistics.

- [Digital Marketing Institute](https://digitalmarketinginstitute.com/): Offers courses and resources on digital marketing strategies and best practices.

- [U.S. Small Business Administration](https://www.sba.gov/): Provides valuable information and resources for entrepreneurs and small business owners.

- [LegalZoom](https://www.legalzoom.com/): Offers legal services and resources for businesses, including information on business structures and legal documents.

- [Entrepreneur](https://www.entrepreneur.com/): A comprehensive resource for entrepreneurs, offering articles, guides, and insights on various aspects of entrepreneurship.

- [Harvard Business Review](https://hbr.org/): Features

articles and research on business strategy, leadership, and innovation.

- [Digital Trends](https://www.digitaltrends.com/): A technology news and information website covering the latest advancements in the digital world.

- [Blockchain Basics](https://www.investopedia.com/terms/b/blockchain.asp): Learn more about the fundamentals of blockchain technology.

- [Sustainability in Business](https:// www.greenbiz.com/): Explore sustainability trends and practices in business and industry.

These resources will help you stay informed, expand your knowledge, and continue your journey in the digital business landscape.

This text was partially created using OpenAI's GPT-3, a large language generation model. The author then reviewed, edited, and revised the generated draft to their satisfaction and is solely responsible for the final content of the publication.

www.ingramcontent.com/pod-product-compliance
Lightning Source LLC
LaVergne TN
LVHW051536050326
832903LV00033B/4280